The Herding Resource Book:
Tips, Advice and Suggestions for People Learning to Herd with
their Dogs

by Laura De La Cruz

So you have a herding dog and a trainer. Now what?

There is a lot to learn when you start herding that doesn't involve actually learning to herd! This book (hopefully) answers all those other questions.

I hope this helps. I'd like to thank everyone at Take Pen Herding who made suggestions and offer support while I worked on this project.

I dedicated my "Aussie Herding" book to my first Aussie, Itsy. I'm dedicating this book to Joker, the dog that started me in herding. Joker (HTCH/WTCH Magiran Jokers Wild, HXAsd/HIAs, HTADIIIsgdc/HTDIIId/HTDIIs, CD (ASCA & AKC), RE CGC, TDI). Joker did it all, and was the first in so many ways here in S. NM/West Texas. But most importantly, he gave his all and made me who I am today.

So you have a dog and you started herding, now what? Time to get a number!

First, let me be clear, it doesn't matter if you have a pure-bred dog or a rescue. Talented dogs work, it is that simple. However, trialing your talented dog isn't that simple.

In order to get titles in herding, you will need a number, such as a registration or tracking number.

If you have a pure-bred AKC (American Kennel Club) dog, it should have a registration number. You will use that number for herding in AKC and you can use it in AHBA (the American Herding Breed Association). However, you will need to get a "tracking" number if you want to trial in ASCA (Australian Shepherd Club of America). You can also use the ASCA number for AHBA instead of the AKC number if you so desire.

If you have a pure-bred dog that isn't AKC registered, you can apply for a PAL number with AKC. Be sure that you apply for a PAL number and NOT a Canine Partner number!
The link is: https://www.akc.org/reg/ilpex.cfm

Only PAL registered dogs can participate in herding, Canine Partner registered dogs cannot (although they can participate in other events such as Rally and Obedience) in AKC.

The PAL number can be used for AHBA. However, you will still need a tracking number from ASCA for participating in ASCA herding events.

If you do not have an AKC number (of either type), you cannot participate in AKC herding events. However, you can still participate in ASCA and AHBA herding events, if your dog is on the list of approved herding breeds or working breeds with a herding background. Check the rules for both AHBA and ASCA where you can find a list of those breeds (links to the rule books for all venues can be found under "Resources" in this book).

Once you get your ASCA tracking number, you can use that for AHBA.

Finally, AHBA will issue you a number if you don't have either an ASCA number or AKC number.

Herding Terms

Here is a list of the most common herding terms. It should help you as you are learning your sport.

AHBA:
The American Herding Breed Association(www.ahba-herding.org)

AKC:
The American Kennel Club (www.akc.org)

ASCA:
The Australian Shepherd Club of America (www.asca.org)

Approach:
The way the dog moves towards the stock. Calm, smooth movement is best.

Away/Away to me:
Movement of the dog in a counter-clockwise direction.

Balance (balance point):
The point where the dog (at an appropriate distance from the stock) is able to control the direction of the movement of the stock and cover any attempts by the stock to break away. Many dogs will naturally find balance, while others may need help. A good stockdog reads the stock and will work the balance point to either fetch or drive stock.

Bubble:
Every individual animal and group (and handler) will have a "bubble" around them where once it is touched (made contact with), induces movement. The bubble will change frequently.

Come-bye:
Movement of the dog in a clockwise direction. See "go-bye."

Contact:
The point where the dog meets the bubble of the stock and induces and maintains movement.

Draw:

Where the stock are drawn to – such as the pen from which they were released, a gate to pasture, a known food source, other livestock or a water source if they are thirsty.

Drive/Driving:
When the dog takes the stock away from the handler and moves the stock away from the handler. The handler will command the dog to make inside flanks to move the stock (moving the dog to various balance points) or the dog will do this naturally.

Exhaust:
Removing stock from the arena, field, or pen.

Eye:
The intensity of the gaze used by a dog to control livestock. See "loose-eyed" and "strong-eyed."

Fetch:
Fetching happens when the dog brings the stock to the handler, typically after an outrun. A straight line fetch is considered best and should be calm and controlled.

Flanks:
Flanks are directional movements the dog makes to move stock. See "come-bye" and "away." Also see "inside flanks."

Flocking:
Flocking comes from the concept of sheep grouping together. This is instinctive and sheep will almost always try to get back to the flock. Cattle and ducks don't have strong flocking tendencies.

Gather:
When the dog moves to collect the stock and organize them into a group.

Go-bye:
Movement of the dog in a clockwise direction. See "come-bye."

Gripping:
Grabbing or biting at the bodies of stock, appropriate gripping is acceptable when dealing with unruly stock (such as a nose hit or nipping at the heel of cows).

Heading (going to head):
When the dog moves to the front (head) of the stock to control or stop their movement.

Heeling:
When the dog works the stock from behind, often including nipping at the heel of the last animal to encourage movement. Most often seen when working cattle.

Herding Instinct:
The desire to work stock – prey drive can been seen as "I'll go get dinner and kill it," while herding instinct can be seen as "I'll go get dinner, bring it to you and you can kill it." Controlled prey drive responsive to the desires of the handler.

Hold/Holding:
The dog places itself in position to stop movement of the stock, often in front of the handler.

Inside Flanks:
When the dog changes directions to move the stock (moving on various balance points) while driving. These are done in front of the handler instead of behind (such as when fetching).

Keenness:
How much interest a dog may show towards stock.

Leg(s):
A qualifying run. You need x number of qualifying runs to get a title (or championship).

Lift:
After the outrun, the dog will make contact with the stock to move them towards the handler. This is the dog's introduction to the stock and should be calm and smooth. See "outrun."

Line/Line Course:
Refers to bringing stock on a straight line, often through a course.

Loose-eyed:
Loose-eyed dogs are dogs that don't stare at stock. They often look around and may actually seem uninterested at times (out of contact or off contact). Often accompanied by an upright body posture.

Medium-eyed:
Medium-eyed dogs watch the stock frequently, but still don't stare. Also usually accompanied by an upright body posture.

Out of Contact/Off Contact:
When the dog is no longer working the stock, either by being too far away from the stock or not paying attention to the stock.

Outrun:
The movement of the dog to get around the stock in order to gather them and bring to the handler. The outrun ends when the lift begins.

Pen:
A small, typically square, enclosure for holding stock. See "take pen."

Penning:
Putting livestock into a pen.

Presence/Power:
How a dog influences stock. Dogs with power/presence show strong self-confidence and can move stock without force. Good stockdogs learn to increase and decrease their presence/power to meet the different situations they may face.

Read/Rate:
Reading stock is the ability of the handler to understand and anticipate the thoughts, behavior and desires of the livestock so that they can manage the stock. Rating is the ability of the dog to understand and anticipate the thoughts, behavior and desires of the stock.

Redirection:
Giving the dog a new command, typically seen on the outrun when the dog hesitates and is given the direction again to reinforce that the handler indeed wants the dog to go that way.

Settle:
Stock that is calm and relaxed is considered settled.

Shed:
When the dog comes into a group of livestock and separates a set number way from the others, holding them from the group.

Steady Approach:
A dog who moves in calmly and easily upon the stock.

Sticky-eyed:
A strong-eyed dog that becomes stuck in place, staring at the stock.

Strong-eyed:
Strong-eyed dogs watch stock intensely and often have a hard time taking their eyes off the stock. Most often seen in Border Collies and Australian Kelpies. See "sticky-eyed."

Take pen:
A small, typically square, enclosure for holding stock where stock are taken out for use, typically into an arena.

Tending:
A form of herding that involves moving large groups of sheep down roads and into grazes. The dog acts as a mobile fence, working the border of the graze to keep the sheep inside the graze.

USBCHA:
United States Border Collie Handlers' Association (www.usbcha.org)

Wearing:
A side-to-side movement by the dog that helps to keep the livestock grouped. Some dogs wear more than others.

Comparisons of AKC, AHBA & ASCA

	AKC (American Kennel Club)	ASCA (Australian Shepherd Club of America)	AHBA (American Herding Breed Association)
Number of legs to title	3 (under 2 different judges)	2 (under 2 different judges)	2 (under 2 different judges)
Titles (Trials)			
Highest (not including championships)	**Excellent** (HXA, HXB, HXC – depending on whether it was on course A, B or C). Following the initials will be the designation for the stock (s=sheep, d=ducks, c=cattle) Example: HXAd means an advanced herding title on ducks on the A course	**Advanced** (ATD). Following will be the designation for the stock (s=sheep, d=ducks, c=cattle) Example: ATDc means an advanced herding title on cattle	**Level III** (The roman numeral will follow the course designation – HTD, HTAD, HRD, RLF). Following will be the designation for the stock (s=sheep, d=ducks, c=cattle) Example: HTDIIIs means an advanced herding title on the HTD course on sheep
Middle	**Intermediate** (HIA, HIB, HIC) Example: HIBd means an intermediate herding title on ducks on the B course	**Open** (OTD) Example: OTDc means an intermediate herding title on cattle	**Level II** Example: HTADIIs means an intermediate herding title on the HTAD course on sheep

Lowest	**Started** (HSA, HSB, HSC) Example: HSAd means a started herding title on ducks on A course	**Started** (STD) Example: STDc means a started herding title on cattle	**Level I** Example: HRDIs means a started herding title on the Ranch course on sheep
Qualifying score	60 in all three	69 in started/88 in open/adv	63 in Level 1/70 in II and III
Maximum score	100 in all three	100 in started/125 in open/adv	90 in Level 1/100 in II and III
Championship	After earning an Excellent title you must compete on that stock and that course (A, B or C). You need 15 points at that level (often called advanced) and at least 2 first place finishes at that level with at least 3 championship points when earning first place – you then earn your HC.	After completing your advanced title in all three stock (sheep, cattle and ducks) you then earn your WTCH.	After earning a Level III title, you need 10 points. Points are earned by completing a Level III course with a score of at least 80. Of those 10 points, no more than 3 can be on ducks, geese or turkeys. You then earn your HTCH.
Tests - tests are judged on a pass/fail basis	There are 3 tests in AKC: HIT (Herding Instinct Test), HT (Herding Tested) and PT (Pre-Trial Tested).	Currently there aren't any tests in ASCA.	There are 2 tests in AHBA: HCT (Herding Capability Test) and JHD (Junior Herding Dog).
Requirements to compete	9 months old and an AKC registration number.	6 months old and an ASCA tracking number (to get a title). Dogs without numbers can compete but no record of their scores will be made.	9 months old. You can use either your ASCA or AKC number or register with AHBA, but consistency is required in order to track scores.
Misc.	The C course is	ASCA now offers	AHBA has a

the tending course and used with tending breeds such as Briards.	a number of different courses in their arena trials (A, B, C, D, E and F). ASCA also offers a Ranch Dog course, Post-Advanced (PTAD) course, and Farm Dog course.	number of courses: HTD – Herding Trial Dog course HTAD – Herding Trial Arena Dog HRD(4 different courses) – Herding Ranch Dog RLF – Ranch Large Flock.
	You can start at any level in AKC but once you get a qualifying score, you can't go back down.	All dogs must start with Started and move up through qualifying and titling.	You can start at any level in AHBA but once you get a qualifying score, you can't go back down.

Tips, Advice and Resources

Tips

You will learn to herd with a trainer. However, there are other things you should know that will help make your life easier. Here are some tips:

1. Get the herding rules for any venue you intend to participate in and read them! Links to the AKC, ASCA and AHBA rules are included in the "Resources" section of this book.

2. Find a good trainer. Look for an experienced trainer. Ask about their experience, number of titles put on dogs, types of dogs, training philosophy and most importantly, watch them work their own dogs.

3. Look for clinics. Those are offered by experienced trainers and you have the opportunity to learn even more! If it is full, ask if you can audit - you can still learn!

4. Have fun! This sport should be fun for you AND your dog. If you ever find yourself not having fun, stop! Take a break and come back to it later. Remember, the dog you go into the arena or pen with is the same dog you are going home with - love them for trying!

Advice

Here is some advice from those who have "been there and done that" for herding newbies!

Cari Hutcheson, Las Cruces, NM: Be patient and build trust between you and your dog. This sport is truly a partnership.

Narita Siegel, Willcox, AZ: Get a good trainer, one you like and respect (I did). Volunteer at trials! Particularly ask if you can time for the judge - you will learn a great deal that way. Listen to what people say and watch how they handle their dogs.

Jeanmarie Beauchat, El Paso, TX: There is no crying in herding!!!

Yvette Misquez, Alamogordo, NM: A must is basic obedience training such as sit, stay and wait.

Joan Morgan, El Paso, TX: Your dog will be a lot smarter than you for a long time.

Terry Kenney, TASK Farms Herding, Training and Trialing Facility: Remember that your herding partner was born with its instinct, your herding skill is an acquired one. Be patient, trust your dog and get good instruction.

Glenda Orman, Burnet, TX: Let your dog work!

Margaret Baxter, Tombstone, AZ: Start training as a puppy, make it a game by teaching the basic down and come.

Sandy Smarsh, Tucson, AZ: Herding is like dancing, when you get in the flow, it is magic.

Mary Weir, Albuquerque, NM: Learn about livestock first!!!

Reegan Ray, San Diego, CA: The purpose of competition herding is to exhibit the relationship man and dog have forged to successfully move, manage and care for livestock. Competition herding exemplifies one of the most important things the dog has contributed to man . . . Moving and protecting his protein source. The relationship you build with a dog in competition herding is unlike that which you find in training for any other sport. It is harder than training for any other work you will do with a dog, and the most satisfying.

Mags Viverito, Orlando, FL: Go to trials and volunteer to be a scribe or timer. Listen to what the judge says. When at a trial watch the stock. Learn to read them. One of the most difficult parts of herding is understanding and reading stock.

Nancy Greenwood: Find a trainer that understands how your breed should work and train it accordingly.

William Sweeney: Be prepared to realize that you are the weak link and have a lot to learn, be open to other more experienced people, and make sure you are having fun! Also learn about the stock, spend time moving stock without a dog, it will help you to understand more about how a dog will make them move.

Cindy Franks: It helps to work stock by yourself - without your dog, in all sorts of areas, then try working a human playing your dog and see how hard it is! Or being the "dog" and having to do what the human is telling you to do.

Ashley W, Washington: Go watch as many trainers as you can. Before putting your dog under them, see what they are like with other dogs, with the stock and the depth of training techniques. If there are some that know your breed, all the better.
Remember there are loose-eyed, upright breed and eye breeds. The two do not work the same.
Most all remember that herding isn't really about you and the dog. It should first and foremost be about the stock. If you want to be good at herding you have to spend time studying stock. You have to care about the stock. Ultimately your dog is a tool, a well-loved tool, but a tool to manage stock calmly, efficiently, and with as little stress to the stock as possible. Even if you only ever plan to do competitive herding, it is always about the stock.

Diana Land: Find a good dog with lots of natural instinct and ability (preferably from herding bloodlines) and find the best trainer you can.

So you entered a trial

So you have been training hard and are getting ready for your first trial. What do you need to know? Here is some advice and a few tips before you head out!

- Your trainer should help you determine what trial and level you will start with - I recommend not doing this on your own! Trust your trainer to put you in the right spot for you and your dog so you can be successful.

- Bring a sense of humor, huge amounts of patience, and some type of relaxation technique for nerves.

- All trials have a "premium" which describes the details abut the event: location, courses, names of judges, etc. Print it out and read it carefully.

- Make sure you have a printout of the directions to the site. Many trials are held at places that don't show up on a GPS! Do NOT trust the GPS if the printed directions tell you something else!

- Before you go, print out the rules of the venue you are trialing in (AKC,ASCA or AHBA) and the course maps.

- Make a note of the closest veterinarian. This is often listed in the premium.

- Check the weather before leaving. Most trials are outside so you should pack for just about any type of weather.

- Check the time of the handler's meeting - that is when the judge will explain answer questions.

- Try to get to the site about an hour before the handler's meeting so you can get settled and potty your dog.

- Remember, keep your dog on leash and quiet at all times. Pick up after your dog. Bring a bunch of poop bags and keep a couple in your pocket at all times!

- Never let your dog pee on the gate or bales of hay. Ask if there is an area for dogs to potty and/or run.

- Make sure you don't have anything hanging off your dog's collar (the sound can influence stock and isn't allowed in AKC anyway). You may want to consider trialing without a collar, particularly on cattle.

- Check in with the Trial Secretary and get your entry number. The entry number is important. It will be on the score sheet and run order. You have to tell the judge the number before you go in the arena and it helps keep track of your scores.

- The Trial Secretary may have a run order printed out for you. At a minimum, one will be posted at the arena. Your entry number will be on the run order and this will tell you when your turn is coming.

- Typically, the advanced classes go first, intermediate second and started last. At some trials the test classes will go before or after the trial classes.

- Most trials will try to follow the run order, but may not be able to stick completely to the order. Some people will be running multiple dogs and have back-to-back slots. Offer to go before or after them so they can get a break.

- Go to the handler's meeting and ask questions - don't be afraid to let them know it is your first time!

- You should have an opportunity to walk the course and check gates. Do this! Gates are different at all facilities and it helps to know before you get in the arena, exactly how to open and close the gates.

- Once the trial starts, be respectful of those running. Don't get too close to the arena and keep your dogs quiet.

- Be close to the arena when your time is near.

- Watch all the runs before and after you. First it is polite and second you can learn a great deal.

- Know the leash rules for the venue you are trialing in. For example, in AKC you go into the arena and unleash the dog at the gate before heading to the handler's post. It is different in ASCA and AHBA.

- Know your dog and your abilities. Know when to call your run (when to stop the dog and leave the arena). Never sacrifice training for trialing!

- Remember, crazy things can happen at a trial that you have no control over (cat in the arena, extra stock in the arena, stock leaving the arena, planes flying just over you to get a good look!). Try not to get rattled and if you do get nervous, call your run. Trialing should be fun, not terrifying!

- When you get ready for your run, put your leash in your pocket. Don't carry it in your hand (it can be considered a training aid). I highly recommend that you don't make it into a loop and sling it over your neck. I did that once at a trial and a sheep slipped its head through it and almost yanked me off my feet! Sure you look "cool" but is it worth it if you get dragged down the arena by out of control livestock?

- Try to remember to thank your judge and the stock-setters when you are finished. Courtesy is always appreciated!

- When leaving the arena, be sure to leash your dog. The team exiting the arena has right of way so give them a chance to get out (unless there is a gate to enter and a gate to leave).

- Tempting as it is, don't pet your dog until you have leashed up and are leaving the arena. This is particularly important in AKC (for some reason!).

- Praise your dog for trialing while handler-impaired! Remember the dog you leave the arena with is the same dog that went in with you. Nothing that happens in the arena is more important than the bond you have with your dog.

- After each class or at the end of the trial (depends on the venue), awards will be handed out. Be there! Not only to get your scoresheets but to applaud the other participants.

- NEVER (and I mean never!) criticize the judge or another contestant's run. It is just bad sportsmanship. Even judges don't criticize other judges or other runs. Congratulate your competitor's after their runs and never bad mouth their runs. The herding world is pretty small and you will get a reputation pretty quickly - and not a good one!

- Save your scoresheets, particularly those with qualifying scores. Start a notebook and keep the sheets there (you can also put title certificates there as well).

- Thank the judge and shake his/her hand. Remember, they are giving you their opinion of your run and that is valuable. Respect their efforts and even if you think they are wrong, thank them! This is where good sportsmanship comes in and be a graceful winner and a graceful loser.

- Ask the judge if you can take a picture with him/her and your dog (and ribbons). Nice to have the memories later!

- Only post the positive on social media later.

- Trialing can be stressful for both you and your dog. Some dogs stop eating completely when trialing. This isn't a big deal if it is a one-day trial but if it is 3 or 4, it becomes serious. Consider bringing something extra besides kibble for your dog (such as canned chicken) to help keep their strength up.

■ Once you have completed the requirements for a title, you should receive a title certificate from the organization. If you don't receive one within about four to six weeks, contact the organization.

■ One last point - be respectful of the facility holding the event. Keep the place clean, don't change or move anything without asking, thank them at the end.

Resources

Here are a number of resources that will help you as you progress through your herding experience.

AKC:
The AKC Stockdog Rulebook can be found at:
https://images.akc.org/pdf/rulebooks/RG9001.pdf

AHBA:
The AHBA Stockdog Rules can be found at:
http://www.ahba-herding.org/

ASCA:
The ASCA Stockdog Rulebook can be found at:
http://www.asca.org/Portals/0/StockdogRules.pdf

Naturally there are a number of Facebook groups and pages you can join and "like" so I'll recommend one to start. It is a FB group called "Herding Dogs: AKC, AHBA & ASCA Herding Trials and Competitions" and you can message me to join:
https://www.facebook.com/groups/125705387027/

There are also a number of Yahoo groups dedicated to herding. Check for ones that are involved in any aspect of herding (AKC, AHBA or ASCA) or ones specific to your breed (Border Collie, Australian Shepherd, Collie, Briard, Kelpie, etc).

Finally, don't forget to check out some great books on herding. Here are some of my recommendations:

"Herding Dogs: Progressive Training" by Vergil S. Holland

"Stockdog Savvy" by Jeanne Joy Hartnagle

"Herding Dogs: Selecting and Training the Working Farm Dog" by Christine Hartnagle Renna

"Training and Working Dogs for Quiet Confident Control of Stock" by Scott Lithgow

"Top Trainers Talk About Starting a Sheepdog: Training a Border Collie on Sheep and Other Livestock" by Molloy and Nadelman

"The Traveling Herding Teacher" by Vest and Kelly

And finally my book:
"Aussie Herding: Interviews with Top Australian Shepherd Stockdog Trainers" available on Amazon at **http://tinyurl.com/lqhbhdy**

Checklist for Trials

So you have your dog and you are ready to go to a trial. Here is a checklist of things to bring. You might want to have a "go bag" ready with some of these so you save time on packing. You may not need all of these things, but you never know!

- A couple of leashes – both slip and clip style

- A couple of stock sticks – you might want to label these as (believe it or not) they are easy to misplace in the excitement of the trial

- Folding chair – the pocket kind are nice but not necessary

- Camera

- Extra clothes, including socks and hats

- Towels (both people and dog towels)

- Stock gloves

- Utility tape

- Some form of shade like a tent or canopy

- Crate for the dog with bowl and extra bottles of water

- Cooler with drinks for both you and the dog and snacks for during the day (if the site is not offering to sell lunch, bring that too)

- First aid kit that includes antihistamine, eye wash, tweezers, nail clippers, bandages, Neosporin

- Canned pumpkin (the pure kind – great for upset stomachs (the dog, not you), can opener and a spoon and/or anti-diarrheal medicine for the dog

- Poop bags

- Notebook, folder (for putting in scoresheets and ribbons), extra pens

- Wet wipes

- Gum

- All-weather outer clothing – rain gear, boots for mud, insulated overalls for snow, hats for sun, etc.

- Sun screen and bug spray

- Shade cloth for the dog crates

- Dog food and snacks

- Copies of the rule book

- Battery-operated fans

- Waterless shampoo

- Jumper cables

- Back or knee supporters

- Disinfectant spray

- Duct tape

- Hand warmers for cold weather

- Dog's favorite toy

- Your emergency contact info

- Dog's microchip number, current picture of the dog (just in case)

- Extra batteries

- Power strip for the hotel so you can charge all your equipment at one time

Thank you for taking the time to read this book. If you liked it, please consider leaving a review on Amazon.

If you have suggestions for additional information to include in future revisions, please feel free to email them to me at thetakepen@gmail.com.

Author Bio:

Laura has been herding for 9 years and has trained, trialed and/or titled a variety of dogs, including Briards, Bergermascos, Pumis, Border Collies, Aussies, Kelpies, Shelties, Collies, Corgis, ACDs, Rotties, Standard Schnauzers and even a Greater Swiss Mountain dog.

She is both an AKC Herding Judge and an AHBA Herding Judge. Laura owns a Briard, 5 Border Collies, 6 Aussies, 2 Kelpies and an Anatolian Shepherd.
She owns (trained, trialed and titled) the first Herding Champion in the El Paso/Las Cruces area (and the second, third and fourth), the first Double-Herding Champion in the area (and the second, third and fourth), and the first dog to earn an AKC Herding Excellent title in the area (and the second and third and the first to earn 2 HX titles).

Her Border Collie, Star, was the subject of an article in the BCSA "Borderlines" magazine in 2012 and her older Border Collie, Joker, was featured in the Aug/Sept, 2013 Veterans edition of the "Borderlines" as Joker earned his second HX at the age of 11 (fewer than 100 dogs have accomplished that in the history of AKC) in 2013. In 2014 Star did what fewer than 10 dogs have ever done in the history of AKC, and that is earn an HX on Cattle at the age of 10 or over.

Laura is the author of "Aussie Herding: Interviews with Top Australian Shepherd Stockdog Trainers" - available on Amazon.

Laura lives in Chaparral, NM between Las Cruces and El Paso, TX where she owns and operates Take Pen Herding.

Postscript:
Relish every minute you have with your best friend. I lost Joker recently and my life is much darker now.

Good night sweet prince
5/28/02 - 11/15/14

Made in the USA
Lexington, KY
23 March 2016